ARCTIC OCEAN

CHUKCHI SEA

COLLVILLE RIVER

NOATAK RIVER

KOBUK RIVER

KOYUKUK RIVER

• FAIRBANKS

NORTON SOUND

YUKON RIVER

TANANA RIVER

MT. MCKINLEY

SUSITNA RIVER

KUSKOKWIM RIVER

COPPER RIVER

• ANCHORAGE

KUSKOKWIM BAY

NUSHAGAK RIVER

GULF OF ALASKA

JUNEAU

KODIAK ISLAND

PACIFIC OCEAN

GLACIER BAY
NATIONAL PARK & PRESERVE

- 3.2 million acres; roughly the size of Connecticut.
- 7 active tidewater glaciers.
- Deepest point in the bay: 1,410' below sea level.
- More than 400,000 cruise ship passengers annually.
- Largest marine area managed by the National Park Service.

Glacier Bay National Park and Preserve

By Kim Heacox

Alaska Geographic Association
Anchorage, Alaska

Alaska Geographic thanks Glacier Bay National Park and Preserve for their assistance in developing and reviewing this publication. Alaska Geographic works in partnership with the National Park Service to further public education and appreciation for national parks in Alaska. The publication of books, among other activities, supports and complements the National Park Service mission.

Author: Kim Heacox

Photography: © Patrick Frischknecht/AccentAlaska.com, 2-3; © Kevin Schafer/AccentAlaska.com, 10; @ Josh Roper/AccentAlaska.com: 16-17; © Steve Bly/AccentAlaska.com: 29; Hugh Rose/AccentAlaska.com, 30-31, 32-33; Kim Heacox/AccentAlaska.com, 48-49, 50-51, 56, 61; Nikolay Konyukhov/AccentAlaska.com, 54; Pat Costello/AccentAlaska.com, inset left 64; © Alaska State Library-Historical Collections, Edward S. Curtis: 22; © Bob Armstrong/naturebob.com: inset middle 64; © Tom & Susan Bean: 8; © Carr Clifton/carrclifton.com: 4-5; © Jon Cornforth/cornforthimages.com: cover, 20, 23, 41, 64-65; © John L. Dengler: 14, inset 48; © Dreamstime.com: inset left 31, inset middle 47; © Kim Heacox: 15, 25, inset right 31, 38, inset top 47; © Fred Hirschman: IV-V, VIII-1, 6, 18-19, 26, 34-35, 36, 52, 53, 57, 58, 59, 66-67, chapter icon Heart, chapter icon Home, chapter icon Rebirth, chapter icon Resilience; © John Hyde/wildthingsphotography.com: inset right 64; © Mark Kelley/markkelley.com: 43, inset bottom 47; © QT Luong/terragalleria.com: 62; © Mint Images/Art Wolfe: VI-VII; © National Park Service: 44-45, 55, 60; © Sean Neilson/seanneilson.com: 13, 24, 28, inset middle 31, inset left 49, inset right 49; © Purestock/Alamy: 27; © Brenda Tharp/brendatharp.com: 46-47; John Muir Papers, Holt-Atherton Special Collections, University of the Pacific Library © Muir-Hanna Trust: 7; © University of Washington Libraries, Special Collections, Harriman 10: 12; © University of Washington Libraries, Special Collections, LaRoche 1170: 9; © University of Washington Libraries, Special Collections, NS3945: 37; © University of Washington Libraries, Special Collections, NA2890: 39; © Brian Wallace: 40.

Map Illustration: Denise Ekstrand
Graphic Design: Eric Cline, TerraGraphica
Editor: Susan Tasaki
Project Managers: Lisa Oakley, Jill Brubaker
Agency Coordinator: Tom VandenBerg, Glacier Bay National Park and Preserve
ISBN: 978-0-9825765-9-5

www.akgeo.org

Alaska Geographic is the official nonprofit publisher, educator, and supporter of Alaska's parks, forests, and refuges. Connecting people to Alaska's magnificent wildlands is at the core of our mission. A portion of every book sale directly supports educational and interpretive programs in Alaska's public lands. Learn more and become a supporting member at www.akgeo.org

Library of Congress Cataloging-in-Publication Data
Heacox, Kim.
Glacier Bay National Park and Preserve / by Kim Heacox.
p. cm.
ISBN 978-0-9825765-9-5
1. Glacier Bay National Park and Preserve (Alaska) 2. Natural history—Alaska—Glacier Bay National Park and Preserve. I. Title.
F912.G5H427 2012
979.8'2--dc23

2012003043

3rd Printing, March 2020

A Place of Discovery

GLACIER BAY NATIONAL PARK AND PRESERVE

Contents

Wildness

On a cold, dreary day in October 1879, while Europe and the United States focused on a future brimming with industrial wonder and promise, new railroads crossed continents and steamships plowed the oceans. A dugout cedar canoe carrying six men entered another America, one deep in the misty past, far to the northwest, roughly one thousand miles north of Seattle. A bay, near as the men could tell. That's what it was. They were paddling into a bay embraced by tall, snowy mountains that climbed into thick clouds, a somber place in some respects, filled with ice and rain and strong currents. But also an exciting place filled with another kind of promise: a land and sea of revelations, discoveries and great possibilities.

The canoe moved with speed and agility. Not surprising, as the main paddlers were four Tlingit Indians who came from the Fort Wrangell region, some 200 miles to the south. Strong, tough, weather-wise men. This was their home, the coastal rainforest country of Alaska where their people had lived for centuries. The bay itself was a remembered landscape that had fed and nourished the Huna Tlingit for countless generations before the great glacier advanced from the north and forced them to move. Now, here it was again, unveiled by the retreating glacier, different but the same,

raw and ice-chafed in the throes of rebirth as it emerged from its frozen sarcophagus. Would life return to the bay as it had before? Would it be bountiful again?

The fifth man in the canoe was a Presbyterian missionary. Like the four Tlingits, he may have had his doubts as to why exactly they were plunging so deep into this intimidating country. Deeper into the wind, cold and rain, deeper into the frigid air and ice-choked waters. He no doubt kept his Bible nearby and said a prayer or two. All five deferred to the sixth man, the bearded, blue-eyed, Scottish-born Californian who exhorted them onward. He had come from "the Yosemite," he said, to see glaciers first-hand. To find out how they worked, how they shaped the land, how they enchanted and created entire worlds.

The head geologist of the state of California had called this man a "mere ignoramus" for declaring that Yosemite Valley was shaped over the millennia not by cataclysmic down-faulting (earthquakes, tectonics and so forth) as the geologist claimed, but by glaciers. What rubbish, the geologist said. How could ice carve rock? How could a glacier—a river of frozen water—cut, shape and sculpt granite? This blue-eyed upstart had no scientific credentials, no proof or gravitas.

That would change. Everything would change. The bay into which the six men paddled in 1879 was a crucible of change, a place where change itself is the only constant, where everything is on its way to becoming something else. Where life finds a way, and no individual, process, seed or idea should be underestimated.

Here, anything seems possible. Coastal brown bears swim five miles across open water, wolverines traverse snow-covered glaciers thousands of feet above sea level, loons call and wolves howl, and lone kayakers paddle into the wind and sleep on the ground. It's a place where three-hundred-pound halibut share nutrient-rich waters with forty-ton humpback whales, sea lions fish for salmon, sea otters feast on urchins and clams, and mountain goats negotiate cliffs. And where, on any given summer day, a thousand cruise-ship passengers stand before a blue tidewater glacier, listening to the ice and birds and their own hearts, separate but the same, beating as one.

This is Glacier Bay, a homeland, a national park, a biosphere reserve, and a world heritage site. A place to lose yourself and find yourself and lose yourself again, to explore deeply but also lightly— with gratitude, curiosity and a healthy sense of wonder. Not an Alaska for the taking, but an Alaska for the saving.

This is the gift we receive from those who came before, the gift we accept with wisdom, restraint, and a promise to pass it on as we received it.

Real freedom lies in wildness, not in civilization.
    — Charles Lindbergh

Rebirth

Glaciers, back in their cold solitudes, work apart from men, exerting their tremendous energies...then they shrink and vanish like summer clouds.

— John Muir

Alaska in 1879 was not unknown. Twelve years earlier, U.S. Secretary of State William Seward, a dedicated expansionist inspired by presidents Thomas Jefferson and Andrew Jackson, masterminded its purchase from Russia for $7.2 million. "Seward's Icebox" and "Seward's Folly," cried a critical press. Just as America was beginning a long reconstruction after a devastating civil war that cost more than a half-million American lives, what did the government do? Buy Alaska from despotic Russia. Not just any Alaska, but a used-up Alaska, plundered by the Tsar's men and their Aleut servants who spent 126 years (from 1741 to 1867) hunting sea otters and leaving nothing. What good could Alaska ever bring to the United States of America?

Inspiration and gratitude, according to the glacier-seeker in the bow of the canoe that entered the bay in 1879. His name was John Muir. And while in his day, some ridiculed him and regarded him as a kook and a crank, they could not deny his outspoken passion for the protection of wild lands—a passion that would soon change the maps and national conscience of America.

He had with him a rough map drawn by Lieutenant Joseph Whidbey, who had charted this coastline under the command of Captain George Vancouver on the HMS *Discovery* in 1794. How different it was then, Muir could see. In Whidbey's time, 85 years earlier, the bay didn't exist. It was filled by a glacier that Whidbey, having no idea what he was looking at, called a "snow cliff," a single massive body of ice that descended from mountains to the north and filled the entire region. So preoccupied were the British with finding the fabled Northwest Passage (a commercially viable sea route over the top of North America) that every time they encountered a massive wall of snow and ice, they assumed it was part of the so-called "Polar Front," a continuous expanse of ice reaching all the way down from the North Pole.

It was not.

Seeing with Different Eyes

Muir had different eyes, mountain vision. He knew what he was looking at: an alpine glacier fed by tributary glaciers to the north, so large that it descended from the mammoth mountains and reached all the way to the sea. Once there, great columns of ice broke away from the tidewater terminus of the glacier and crashed into the ocean, filling the inlets with icebergs. Like so much else in nature, the glacier oscillated. It had cycles. Over centuries and millennia, it advanced and retreated again and again, sometimes burying and then unveiling entire landscapes in a short period of time.

John Muir as a young man in 1860. His first trip to Alaska was 19 years later.

Muir's companions, the four Tlingit paddlers, knew this as a world defined by change, and by water in its many forms: ice, snow, rain, rivers, streams, tides, clouds, glaciers, estuaries, lakes, coves, inlets, violent storms and gentle mists, a thousand expressions seen and unseen. These men knew every cove and stream and meadow—places that had names before the glacier last advanced and evicted the ancestors of the Huna Tlingit, probably in the late 1600s, during the peak of what we today call the Little Ice Age. The great glacier completely filled the bay for perhaps a half century (from roughly 1700 to 1750), then began a catastrophic retreat. What Whidbey recorded on his map was the beginning of one of the most rapid glacial retreats in recorded history. Eighty-five years later, Muir found a bay half-unveiled. He named it Bay of Great Glaciers.

"The Master Builder chose for a tool," Muir wrote, "not the thunder and lightning to rend and split asunder, not the stormy torrents, nor the eroding rain, but the tender snowflake, noiselessly falling through unnumbered generations."

Feeding the Glaciers

To the west and north of Glacier Bay, the Fairweather Range and Saint Elias Mountains rank among the tallest coastal mountains in the world, with peaks rising 15,000 and 18,000 feet above sea level. Storms and heavy weather lash these mountains, blowing in from the Gulf of Alaska and feeding glaciers with the only food they need, the only food that makes them grow: snow. This country receives roughly 75 inches of rain annually at sea level (measured at Cape Spencer).

When it rains at lower elevations, it snows up high, layer upon layer building up, the weight of overlying snow compressing the older, deeper layers far below. Over time, the snow recomposes into firn, a snow/ice intermediate stage, and recrystalizes further into dense glacial ice. But not the same kind of ice that sits in little trays in your freezer and cools your drink. That ice forms from

water quick-cooled under no pressure. Glacial ice is different. It's recrystalized snow, has greater density and is not uniformly the same—it can be thicker in some parts than in others and, as a result of the way light interacts with it, is more blue. A glacier can also have more overburden (rocks and sediment) in one area than another. All of this fascinated John Muir, who came to Alaska to find large, magnificent glaciers, not gold; to find trees, not timber; to find the better part of himself in the tonic of wildness. He wasn't disappointed.

"A Shrieking, Vitriolic Blue"

On his third visit to Glacier Bay, in 1890, John Muir built and occupied a cabin at Muir Point, near the tidewater face of his namesake glacier, and answered questions from tourists who came to the area on sidewheelers—similar to questions asked of park rangers on cruise ships today—including, "Why is the ice blue?"

The technical answer: The color is the result of the interaction of light and crystals. In dense glacial ice, all wavelengths of the visible light spectrum are absorbed except blue, which is refracted and scattered.

Muir called it a "shrieking, vitriolic blue," and said, "If you were as cold as the glacier, you'd be blue too."

The view of Muir Glacier in 1893 from the shoulder of Mount Wright. Today, the view is quite different. Where the glacier once stood is now the waters of Muir Inlet. To see glaciers from this spot today, one would need binoculars.

"Why does Muir climb mountains in the middle of a storm?" the Tlingits asked while warming themselves around a fire. They were camped on the west side of Glacier Bay, a short distance north of what today is Geikie Inlet.

"To seek knowledge," answered their traveling companion, Samuel Hall Young, the Presbyterian missionary.

Muir had taken off in a cold, wind-driven rain to see what he could find, and find what he could see. Nothing was missed in his careful observations.

He returned to camp that night, he said, "wet, weary and glad." Climbing high up a mountain flank, he had caught a glimpse of five great glaciers coalesced into one, obscured by clouds but visible nonetheless. Muir would later describe a similar scene as an "icy wildness unspeakably pure and sublime."

Surging Forward, Falling Back

We travel down the road of mystery to gain knowledge. But also, and perhaps just as important, we travel down the road of mystery to deepen the mystery.

The bay Muir and company paddled into was a landscape of rebirth, coming back to life after a long, icy slumber. The great glaciers in front of him were in retreat, shrinking back into their mountain lairs, beginning to splinter into smaller tributary streams of ice.

How and why glaciers advance and retreat was, in Muir's time, just beginning to be understood. Today, we know that a glacier, driven by gravity, flows forward, much like a river flows forward. But a glacier flows forward only so far. Sooner or later, it ends. As it descends to lower elevations and warmer temperatures, it loses ice from its terminus at a rate equal to or faster than its rate of flow.

Like a bank account, a glacier has a system of pluses and minuses. Snow falls at high elevations, in what is called the zone of accumulation, at or near the source of the glacier, and is recrystallized into glacial ice. That ice travels down slope and disappears from the lower reaches of the glacier, where it melts and fractures off in what is called the zone of ablation. (Only tidewater glaciers, which are rare, are said to "calve" their ice at their terminus.)

Think of it as a zone of deposits at the top and a zone of withdrawals at the bottom. If a glacier receives a tremendous amount of snow up high, and the snow is held at cold temperatures and effectively recrystallized into glacial ice, the glacier is healthy. Deposits are strong. It can move forward with vigor and enthusiasm, and perhaps advance, as many glaciers have over the long history of the Earth. But if snowfall decreases, or temperatures warm up, and rain (instead of snow) falls at higher elevations, the zone of ablation increases, melting accelerates and the glacier retreats. The rate of withdrawal outpaces the rate of deposit. The terms "advance" and "retreat" apply to the position of the glacial terminus, but also offer a way to assess the overall health of a glacier. A retreating glacier still flows forward, but loses ice off its terminus at a rate faster than its rate of flow, as the overall length of the glacier decreases. As the glacier retreats, it shrinks, losing ice mass throughout its entire length, width and breadth. A good example of this is the Mendenhall Glacier, near the Juneau Airport.

While most glaciers in Alaska and throughout the world today are in a state of retreat, a few in Glacier Bay receive new snow at high elevations in the Fairweather Range and remain healthy, holding their positions in a warming world. The Johns Hopkins and Gilman glaciers even show occasional signs of advancing. How this would thrill John Muir.

"Man, man, you ought to have been with me," he once told Missionary Young upon returning from an adventure on a glacier. "You'll never make up for what you have lost today. I've been wandering through a thousand rooms of God's crystal temple. I've been a thousand feet down in the crevasses, with matchless domes and sculpted figures and carved ice-work all about me.

Solomon's marble-and-ivory palaces are nothing to it. Such purity, such color, such delicate beauty. I was tempted to stay there and feast my soul, and softly freeze, until I would become part of the glacier. What a great death that would be."

Camelot Afloat

Muir returned to Glacier Bay three more times: 1880, 1890 and, finally, as a distinguished member of the Harriman Expedition of 1899, when he was 61 and the most famous preservationist in America. (Four years later, he would host President Teddy Roosevelt in Yosemite, and break away with Roosevelt to go camping on Granite Point.) Always keen to listen and learn, Muir signed the Harriman guest register as an "author and student of glaciers."

Accompanying him was a nineteenth-century think tank of America's "genteel tradition," a Camelot afloat composed of the most illustrious scientific experts, artists, photographers and literary men in the country, plus the expedition's benefactor, Edward H. Harriman, president of the Union Pacific Railroad. For two months, the expedition traveled from Seattle to Nome and back, exploring a vast stretch of Alaska coastline. They spent more time in Glacier Bay—five days—than in any other location. Edward S. Curtis took photographs. George Bird Grinnell (editor of *Field & Stream*) and C. Hart Merriam (director of the US Biological Survey) discussed conservation. Henry Gannett and Grove Karl Gilbert studied glaciers and rocks. Louis Agassiz Fuertes painted birds. John Burroughs, America's premier nature writer, composed letters and essays.

The Harriman Expedition of 1899 traveled on the George W. Elder, a steamer specially refurbished with scientific labs and to provide comfort for its scholarly passengers. This was no ordinary cruise to Alaska. Onboard were numerous scientists, artists, photographers, and writers, many of which later became significant figures in science, art and conservation.

McBride Glacier (upper left) calves into the frigid waters of McBride Inlet, and ice jams along a spit at the inlet's mouth. Forty years earlier, McBride Glacier occupied the entire length of the inlet.

Snow falls every month of the year in the higher elevations of the Fairweather Range, where layer upon layer recrystallizes into dense glacial ice.

How fondly Muir remembered his first trip into the bay 20 years before, in the canoe with his missionary friend S. Hall Young and the four remarkable Tlingit paddlers: Toyatte, a Stickeen nobleman and captain of the canoe, imposing and seawise; Kadichan, son of a Tlingit chief and a great orator and expert on Tlingit protocol; Sitka Charley, a fine hunter; and Stickeen John, a capable interpreter.

A Future in the Balance

Already, those days seemed distant to Muir, representative of a time lost, as gold-seekers poured into Alaska by the tens of thousands. "It was the end of a different age, with different mores," wrote historians William H. Goetzmann and Kay Sloan in their acclaimed book, *Looking Far North*, "though it would be too simple to term it, as some have, an Age of Innocence. Rather, it was an age of strange binocular vision that was at times replete with irony. Essentially, the Harriman expeditioners saw two Alaskas—one, the stunning, pristine land of forests and mountains and magnificent glaciers, the other, a last frontier, being invaded . . . by [those with] false dreams of success."

The future of Glacier Bay lay in the balance. Would it become an Alaska for the saving, or for the taking? A place to celebrate gold, or glaciers? Most gold hounds had bypassed Glacier Bay en route up Lynn Canal to Skagway and Dyea, the jumping-off points for the Klondike goldfields farther north. But what of other temptations?

"Nothing dollarable is safe," wrote Muir.

He had given us another America, a second chance, one still wet with dew and open to new sensibilities. He had described Alaska not as a place of daunting cold but of magnificent beauty. And let us not forget, he added, that there are times when beauty is as important as bread, and more nourishing for the soul. ■

Brown bears work the beaches when the tide is low turning over rocks looking for tasty barnacles, clams and other intertidal life.

Flowing Ice,
Shaping Landscapes

How can ice carve rock? How do glaciers shape the land? These were vexing questions in the mid-1800s, when glaciology was a young science and geologists were just beginning to comprehend the age of the Earth and the consequences of small processes long continued. If glaciers indeed sculpt and chisel landscapes, and pulverize bedrock into silt, how do they do it? (Muir was not the first to propose that glaciers were responsible for this type of erosion. In 1837, Louis Agassiz, one of his mentors, had made these same observations.)

It turns out that ice is not the chisel, it's the hand on the chisel. Ice is too soft to cut rock. Instead, glaciers pick up rocks of all sizes and grind them against the bedrock. But how, exactly?

Glaciers flow. They are rivers of ice always on the move; some faster than others, some with more power. On the surface, they tend to be brittle. When they flow down steep slopes or around sharp topographic turns, they often fracture into a bewitching hatchwork of crevasses and tall towers of ice called seracs. Deep down, however, where the basement ice is under great pressure from the immense weight of the overlying ice, the glacier is more "flexible." Where the belly of the glacier rubs against bedrock, the pressure can be so great that the ice melts and lubricates the ice/rock interface, giving it flexibility and allowing it to slip and slide past rocky obstacles. When the pressure releases and the ice refreezes, the glacier picks up small pieces of rock, which become embedded in the ice.

The glacier flows onward, now with a rock in its grip, and grinds this rock against the bedrock. At any given time, an active glacier can have thousands—maybe millions—of rocks embedded in its margins, grinding away at the bedrock like a massive piece of cold sandpaper. Added up over the millennia, this process can profoundly reshape the land, just as multiple generations of artists, working with chisels and making one strike at a time, can reshape stone.

As glaciers move down slope, plucking and grinding along their edges, they undercut the flanks of mountains, sometimes causing a landslide of stones onto the ice and creating features called lateral moraines, dark bands of rock and sediment on the glacier's surface margins. Where two glaciers flow together, like two tributaries joining and becoming a larger river, the lateral moraines fuse into a medial moraine, a dark stripe down the middle of the larger glacier.

A close look at the surface of many glaciers reveals that they're not as clean as you might expect. They're peppered with rocks, boulders, gravel and pockets of silt, sediments of all sizes that geologists call overburden. A glacier is both an agent of erosion and of deposition, carrying materials from higher elevations and dropping them at lower elevations.

Resilience

The question is not what you look at, but what you see.
 —Henry David Thoreau

Life finds a way. Scrape the earth clean, right down to bedrock, scour it of all visible signs of life—every seed, spore and vestige of soil—and life will return. Maybe not right away. And probably not as it was before in every detail and design. But it will find a way. In the aftermath of glacial retreat or a massive volcanic eruption that destroys entire forests and fertile valleys, the land becomes green again, in time. It's a process scientists call "primary plant succession." In 1916, it was little understood.

That summer, while Europe consumed itself in a brutal war, William S. Cooper, a soft-spoken, bespectacled ecologist from the University of Minnesota, arrived in Glacier Bay with a few questions and a quiet determination. He aimed to discover how succession worked; how the land changed; how, again and again after a glacier or volcano has sterilized an entire region, the land could prove wondrously resilient.

Little did he know that he was resilient himself; that he, too, would change and become someone he'd never been before: a conservation activist. Little did he know that what he would do for Glacier Bay, it would in turn do for him: make him into something much more than what he'd been. And little did he know that the newly created National Park Service, born that same summer of 1916, would one day administer the land and sea he was about to adopt and fight for—first as a national monument; then as a national park and biosphere reserve; and finally as part of an international World Heritage Site that, at 25 million acres, is the largest contiguous array of preserved land in the world outside of the Antarctic.

Landscape as Textbook

Cooper established nine vegetation quadrats that summer, all in places where he knew the exact date of ice recession—when the land had become exposed to open air, sunshine, rain and ecological processes for the first time in hundreds, perhaps thousands, of years after its entombment under the great glacier. In 1921, he returned and recharted the quadrats by way of compass bearings, cairns, pacings and white crosses on rocks. He meticulously measured the growth and distribution of plants large and small, from Sitka spruce to miniature mosses. In Muir Inlet, he made a thorough analysis of interstadial stumps, the mysterious remains of ancient forests: trees that had grown in the upper bay thousands of years before and had been partially buried in deep deposits, then sheared off by advancing glaciers. For Cooper, as it had been for John Muir, all these clues were a small part of a larger text eloquently written on the land by Nature.

Plant succession presented itself as a series of plant communities, one after another, the earliest ones pioneering new ground. Over the decades, each community displaced the one that came before, beginning with lichens on bare rock, advancing to mosses, then small vascular plants. Woody plants followed, such as willow and Sitka alder, that fixed atmospheric nitrogen in the soil and made the land suitable for the final stage: Sitka

The Antiquities Act

It's been called "the greatest conservation act nobody's ever heard of." In 1872, Congress established the first national park in Yellowstone. Some proposed parks, starved by stalemate, never made it into law. Even worse, by the early 1900s, souvenir hunters were vandalizing archeological sites throughout the Southwest. In 1906, Congressman John F. Lacey sponsored a bill known today as the Antiquities Act, which enabled the president to create a national monument by executive order, with a stroke of the pen. No congressional approval necessary. Teddy Roosevelt took the act and ran with it, establishing many large national monuments that later became national parks. Inspired by Roosevelt, Calvin Coolidge used the act in 1925 to establish Glacier Bay National Monument.

spruce and western hemlock, great evergreen trees that eventually towered over the alders, robbed them of light, and contributed to their demise.

In turn, each successive community of plants provided new habitat for insects, birds and mammals, a moving tapestry of wildlife, tides of wild creatures flowing into new riches and competing for space and food, finding every opportunity to feed and reproduce and play the game of survival.

From the forested lower bay to the barren upper bay, where the glaciers still dwelled at the heads of their rock-ribbed inlets, Cooper could see that a trip through Glacier Bay was a trip through more than geography. It was a trip through time, a journey back into the ice age, from green forests in the lower bay (where the ice had been absent the longest) to blue glaciers in the upper bay (where ice still reigned). The entire bay was a magnificent living laboratory, a scientific bonanza.

What the Grand Canyon was to geology, Glacier Bay was to ecology. A textbook, an elegant stratification of sorts. But rather than being laid out vertically as it was in the Grand Canyon, here it presented itself horizontally, over the entire 70-mile length of the bay, a perfect place to better understand nature's hidden processes.

Monument First, Park to Follow

In Boston, at the annual meeting of the Ecological Society of America in late 1922, Cooper shared his discoveries with his fellow scientists. Barrington Moore, former president of the society, recommended that the Glacier Bay region be protected as a national park or monument. Robert F. Griggs, who had played a key role in the 1916 discovery of the Valley of Ten Thousand Smokes (created by the 1912 eruption of Novarupta Volcano on the Alaska Peninsula, due west of Kodiak Island) and the establishment of Katmai National Monument, agreed with Moore.

This 1899 photograph taken near Muir Glacier shows a forest of interstadial stumps. These broken trees are the remains of an ancient forest that was destroyed by a previous advance of ice. Erosion continues to expose these ghostly remains throughout Glacier Bay.

As glaciers retreat, the land is renewed. First lichen then flowers, such as these river beauty and Indian paintbrush, grow in the newly created soil. In time, even trees return to the land. Virtually all the vegetation in Glacier Bay has returned in the past 300 years following the retreat of its glaciers, making the park one of the premier sites on the planet to study plant recolonization.

Against a backdrop dominated by Brady Glacier and the tallest peaks of the Fairweather Range (upper left), the upper arms of Dundas Bay reach deep into mountain topography. It was on Brady Glacier that John Muir had his harrowing 1880 adventure with the little dog Stickeen.

He wrote, "A national monument is created by presidential proclamation, whereas a national park is made by an act of Congress. In the first case it is necessary only to convince one man of the advisability of the action, while in the second, 600, more or less, must be converted to the idea."

Cooper, Barrington and Griggs were men of science, not avarice. They had enough money. What they wanted was the preservation of wild nature for human knowledge and inspiration, places that would hold forever the answers to questions humans had not yet learned to ask. Often in their writings, they capitalized the word "Nature" as Muir had, as if those American places still vast and wild were their church, or if not a church, then at least deserving of some special sacredness.

It took Charles Sheldon and Belmore Browne nearly ten years of unrelenting letter-writing and visits to Washington to get Congress to finally pass the bill creating Mount McKinley National Park in 1917, the first national park established after the birth of the National Park Service. (In 1980, the park would be tripled in size and renamed Denali National Park and Preserve).

Ten years is a long time. A landscape could be irreparably altered in that span. Look at Niagara Falls, the Florida Keys, Lake Tahoe, Puget Sound, to name a few, all great beauties before the bulldozers arrived. Griggs was right. Get a national monument first; with luck, a park will follow.

But sweeping public land protection is never easy in a consumptive, business-minded, money-is-king culture.

"A monstrous proposition," announced the Juneau *Daily Empire* in 1924, upon hearing of the recommendation to make Glacier Bay a national monument. "It is said the proposed National Monument is intended to protect Muir Glacier and to permit the study of plant and insect life in its neighborhood. It tempts patience to try to discuss such nonsensical performances. The suggestion that a reserve be established to protect a glacier that no one could disturb if he wanted and none would want to disturb if he could or to permit the study of plant and insect life is the quintessence of silliness."

Up until then and ever since, hardly a single national park has been established in the United States without a difficult fight. Yet once established, no national park has been dissolved. Together as a family, or a quilt, the parks become part of our national conscience, our best identity and a reflection of ourselves. Great acts of conservation, like little plants growing in the shadows of glaciers, require their own degree of resilience and toughness, a posture, if not an attitude, of never giving up. It often comes down to one man or one woman, or at most a small band of committed people working together, to change history. "Never doubt that a small group of thoughtful, committed citizens can change the world," observed anthropologist Margaret Mead. "Indeed, it is the only thing that ever has."

Lupine grow in open, deglaciated areas throughout the park's lower elevations up to 5,000 feet.

25

William Cooper returned to Glacier Bay in 1929 and 1935, checked his vegetation quadrats and journeyed far up Muir Inlet. On land freshly exposed by retreating ice, he found interstadial stumps: western hemlocks that (as later determined by carbon dating) had been 400 years old when a glacier had buried them roughly seven thousand years previously. The evidence was obvious. Glacier Bay was once much like it is today, with the glaciers sequestered in their inlets and the surrounding land blanketed in a mature, old-growth forest.

Nature's Ebb and Flow

For thousands of years—millions of years—the ocean has moved, tide-like, as have the mountains, glaciers and forests, through the processes of ice advance and retreat, plant succession, and habitat evolution. The entire bay rocked between waves of destruction and creation: entombed by glaciers, followed by liberation, again by entombment and liberation, over and over. Blankets of ice and blankets of trees, dark and light, the grand processes repeating themselves, the movements of wolves and whales, sea lions and bears.

The process of succession, in all its complexity, isn't limited to the land. It enlivens the sea as well, and every foot of the shore. It bursts with life every summer. Phytoplankton bloom in spring, and continue to bloom well into June and July. Fat-rich forage fish (herring, sand lance, capelin) explode in numbers and provide ample food for humpback whales, sea lions, harbor seals, harbor porpoises and thousands of birds: eagles, terns, gulls, guillemots, cormorants, puffins, murres, murrelets and others. Salmon run up rivers and streams where years before no salmon ran at all. Pods of killer whales come and go. Great rafts of sea otters float off modest islands where 30 years before no sea otters lived. The bay pulses with life.

Sunset view toward Tarr Inlet of the West Arm of Glacier Bay.

Thousands of seabirds nest on the cliffs and rocky shores both within the bay and on the park's outer coast. Black-legged kittiwakes breed in large colonies along the park's steep cliffs, where they lay one or two spotted eggs in a mud nest lined with moss or seaweed.

Fed by tremendous snowfall in the Fairweather Mountains, the Johns Hopkins Glacier extends over 12 miles to reach the sea.

Richness Unmatched

Over the decades, many scientists have followed Cooper's example, dedicating a considerable portion of their professional lives to better understand the heartbeat of Glacier Bay. Take, for example, Greg Streveler, who moved to Gustavus, a small town adjacent to Glacier Bay, as a park biologist in the 1960s. After nearly a half-century here, he believes the lower waters of Glacier Bay, together with Icy Strait (the body of water due south of Glacier Bay), "are perhaps the most biologically productive waters in all of coastal Alaska." That's saying something, as Alaska has more miles of coastline—nearly 34,000—than the entire contiguous U.S.

As chairman of the Alaska Game Board for a couple of years, Streveler traveled all over the state, and saw a lot. A good scientist who's disinclined to exaggerate, he observes that erosion by ice and water washes tremendous amounts of nutrient-rich sediment into Glacier Bay every summer day. Powerful tides ebb and flow through the lower bay and out into Icy Strait, creating strong currents that, together with winds and storms, stir nutrients to the surface. Add abundant sunlight (summer days up to 19 hours long), and the result is a combination that makes for a richness unmatched. Glacier Bay is not only a refuge or a scientific lab—it's a nursery, a place where life and death spin in close radius, and glaciers grind down the rocks that feed the sea and all the organisms that live there.

"Glacier Bay's contribution to the world is as multifaceted as it is enduring," adds Lewis Sharman, an ecologist at the park. "It's a drop-dead gorgeous landscape and seascape that inspires and provides for 're-creation' in its purest sense. It's largely ecologically intact. At the same time, it offers unparalleled 'opportunity value' to research."

The place that gave us a fundamental understanding of primary plant succession, thanks to William Cooper, has inspired scores of researchers to follow his example and contribute many years of their own field time, bringing us, according to Sharman, "a more nuanced and complete exposition of plant succession. . . . But it's the deep impact that Glacier Bay has on its scientists that most impresses me. I see them arrive—both first-timers and returning elders—and I see faces of absolute pure wonder and delight. And I've seen them leave at the end of a field season with tears rolling down their faces. Not tears of sadness or despair, but tears of gratitude and deep satisfaction. As if to say, 'I'll never have my fill, I'll never, ever forget,' and, perhaps most frequently of all, 'I can't wait to come back.' And they do." ∎

Stunted trees highlight the boggy, muskeg ecosystem found in the lowlands near the mouth of Glacier Bay.

A Sampling of
Species

Brown bear	*Ursus arctos*
Black bear	*Ursus americanus*
Wolf	*Canis lupus*
Coyote	*Canis latrans*
Wolverine	*Gulo gulo*
Moose	*Alces alces*
Mountain goat	*Oreamnos americanus*
Beaver	*Castor canadensis*
Porcupine	*Erethizon dorsatum*
River otter	*Lutra canadensis*
Humpback whale	*Megaptera novaeangliae*
Killer whale	*Orcinus orca*
Steller sea lion	*Eumetopias jubatus*
Harbor seal	*Phoca vitulina*
Harbor porpoise	*Phocoena phocoena*
Sea otter	*Enhydra lutris*

Harbor seals (below) give birth on glacier-calved icebergs, where their pups can be nursed in safety from predation by transitory killer whales. In recent years, harbor seal numbers have fallen sharply around Alaska. Seals in Glacier Bay are studied and closely monitored to better understand their breeding and population dynamics. From left: porcupine, river otter, brown bear.

Humpback Whales

Every summer, humpback whales return to the cold, nutrient-rich waters of Glacier Bay to feast on fish, krill and other small prey. They arrive hungry, most of them having made the long journey from their winter breeding and calving grounds in Hawaii, and some in Mexico, where they've fasted for months—both in their wintering areas and during their migrations. A few may have wintered in Alaska.

From 1974 to 2011, approximately 656 humpbacks were identified in the bay, including a few "grandmother" whales with fully grown calves returning as breeding adults with calves of their own. The adult-to-calf ratio has been robust over the years; scientists estimate the central North Pacific humpback whale population growth rate at 5.8 percent. If such a growth rate continues, the population could double in size every 12 years.

People often ask about the weight, length and age of a humpback whale. The numbers vary, of course, given the individual variation within any natural population. But a good rough estimate for an adult humpback whale in Glacier Bay is 35 tons, 45 to 50 feet, and 40 to 60 years (though most adult humpbacks weigh about 1,600 pounds per foot of length, not 2,000 pounds). Their scientific name, *Megaptera novaeangliae*, which means "long-winged New Englander," is apt. A mature humpback has 15-foot-long pectoral flippers (equal to roughly one-third its total body length) that give it great agility. Herman Melville called it "the most gamesome of all whales," given its full repertoire of surface behavior: body breaches, pectoral slaps, spy-hopping, tail-lobbing and lunge-feeding.

Whale biologists identify individual whales from photographs taken of the unique patterns on the underside of their tail flukes, and from analyzing DNA rendered from flakes of skin sloughed off by breaching whales and collected from the surface of the ocean. A hydrophone in Bartlett Cove, near park headquarters, also contributes data on the whales, plus data on vessel noise and how it might alter whale behavior.

While humpbacks were once thought to sing only in their tropical wintering grounds, males have been recorded singing in Glacier Bay in late summer, as though tuning up for their journey south. We're not sure why. Humpback whales are still a mystery to us, which serves to enhance our fascination.

"Regardless of how much time I spend studying whales," says Janet Neilson, a whale biologist in Glacier Bay, "they always surprise me with some aspect of their behavior. Every day on the water with them is truly a privilege."

Many whales documented in the park's whale-monitoring program have been sighted annually since the 1970s. However, as Neilson's colleague, Christine Gabriele, a whale biologist in Glacier Bay since 1991, observes, "Even after decades of careful study, the whales retain much of their mystery. I'm not sure we'll ever fully understand how they navigate, find food and maintain contact with each other in the dark, salty waters of Alaska. Every once in a while, a new piece of the puzzle is revealed, inspiring a renewed interest in filling in the rest of the picture."

We used to slaughter whales for corset boning and oil, now we celebrate them. We celebrate them for all their natural magnificence, mystery and grace. There's no mystery in that, only more reasons to celebrate.

Home

These lands are vital not only to our subsistence, but also to our
sense of being as Tlingit people.
—Gabriel George. Tlingit fisherman

The French explorer Jean-François de Galaup, comte de Lapérouse, was a long way from home in 1786 when his two frigates, *Astrolabe* and *Boussole*, sailed on a flood tide through tricky currents and past treacherous rocks into Lituya Bay. Due east of his position, beyond the imposing peaks we today call the Fairweather Range, was Glacier Bay, though when Lapérouse arrived, it was nearly all glacier and no bay.

The Tlingit elder he greeted in Lituya Bay stood rooted and secure, entirely at home in this wild, ice-cut, storm-tossed world. He and his people's ancestors knew this place well. Like Lapérouse, who had been a sailor for 30 years, the elder was a son of the sea. But rather than travel by ship, he traveled by canoe, as did all his people—men, woman and children alike. So comfortable were Tlingit youngsters in canoes that they looked to the French as if they'd been born with paddles in their hands.

"On occasions of high ceremony," Lapérouse wrote of the Tlingit men, "they wear their hair long, braided and powdered with the down of sea fowl. A simple skin is thrown over their shoulders." while their heads "they commonly cover with a little straw hat, curiously; though sometimes they wear on their heads caps with two horns, eagle's feathers, and entire heads of bears fitted on a skullcap of wood. These kinds of head-dresses are greatly diversified, but their principal object, like that of most of their customs, is to render them frightful, perhaps to awe their enemies." Lapérouse noticed that when Tlingit women were given presents, they "wished the sun to be witness of their actions, and refused to retire into the woods."

Of the grand beauty of Lituya Bay, and of his time with the Tlingit, Lapérouse wrote, "Not a port in the universe could afford more conveniences for accelerating a business often tedious in other countries. In short, we considered ourselves as the most fortunate of navigators, in having arrived at such a distance from Europe without having had a single person sick, and without an individual of either crew being attacked with the scurvy. But here the greatest of misfortunes, and most impossible to be foreseen, awaited us."

Tlingit ocean-going canoes are structures of beauty and performance for navigating rough seas. This engraving of a Tlingit canoe was made in 1786 during Laperouse's stay in Lituya Bay.

Disaster Strikes

A man of the Enlightenment—a man of books, science, careful observation and keen intelligence—Lapérouse had been away on this particular voyage for nearly a year (he'd left Brest in August 1785), and had a long way yet to go. He intended to circumnavigate the world and conduct great science, achieving for France what James Cook had for Great Britain. Little did he know that revolution was brewing in Paris, the king would soon lose his head and even sooner, his own fate would involve a terrible loss followed by greater loss.

His misfortune was, in fact, not impossible to foresee. The Tlingits had warned him to be careful of tide rips at the entrance to the bay, which he'd entered on a flood tide and seen at its calmest. They spoke gravely about losing seven of eight canoes there not long before.

The day of Lapérouse's arrival, July 4, 1786, happened to be the tenth birthday of the continent's young nation, and was greeted with celebration in the bustling cities of Philadelphia, Boston and New York. In Lituya Bay, a world away, two remarkable cultures regarded one another with careful gestures and goodwill. Taking the Tlingit warning to heart, Lapérouse gave written instructions to his officers, forbidding them to approach the dangerous currents as they pushed off in three boats to measure soundings of the bay. "Do you think me a child?" one officer replied with mild disdain. "I have commanded ships of war."

As if pulled by a magnet, the water beneath the three boats behaved like a vortex. First one boat was sucked into the current and thrown against the breakers, then a second. Only by "the superior construction of his boat and his enlightened prudence," according to Lapérouse, did the commanding officer of the third boat survive being wrecked while he and his crew tried to rescue their fellow sailors.

At the foot of a monument, Lapérouse left a message in a bottle: "At the entrance of this harbour perished 21 brave seamen. Reader, whoever thou art, mingle thy tears with ours."

"The Indians," he later noted, "appeared to participate in our grief, which is extreme."

Shaken, the surviving Frenchmen sailed from Lituya Bay on July 30. Weeks later, on the Kamchatka Peninsula in the Russian Far East, Lapérouse may have had a premonition that he and his expedition would never make it home. He sent his journal and scientific records overland (across Siberia) to Paris, thinking they would have a better chance of survival. It was a prescient decision. From Kamchatka, he sailed south and was never seen again, disappearing, as best we know, in the Vanikoro region of Polynesia.

Carvings in living spruce trees by traditional Tlingit artists serve both as trail markers and as reminders of ancient ties to the land.

Tlingit men and boys pose in ceremonial regalia in Hoonah sometime in the early 1900s. Regalia identifies the wearer's clan and honors their ancestors. The greater the detail and number of ornaments indicates higher status and wealth.

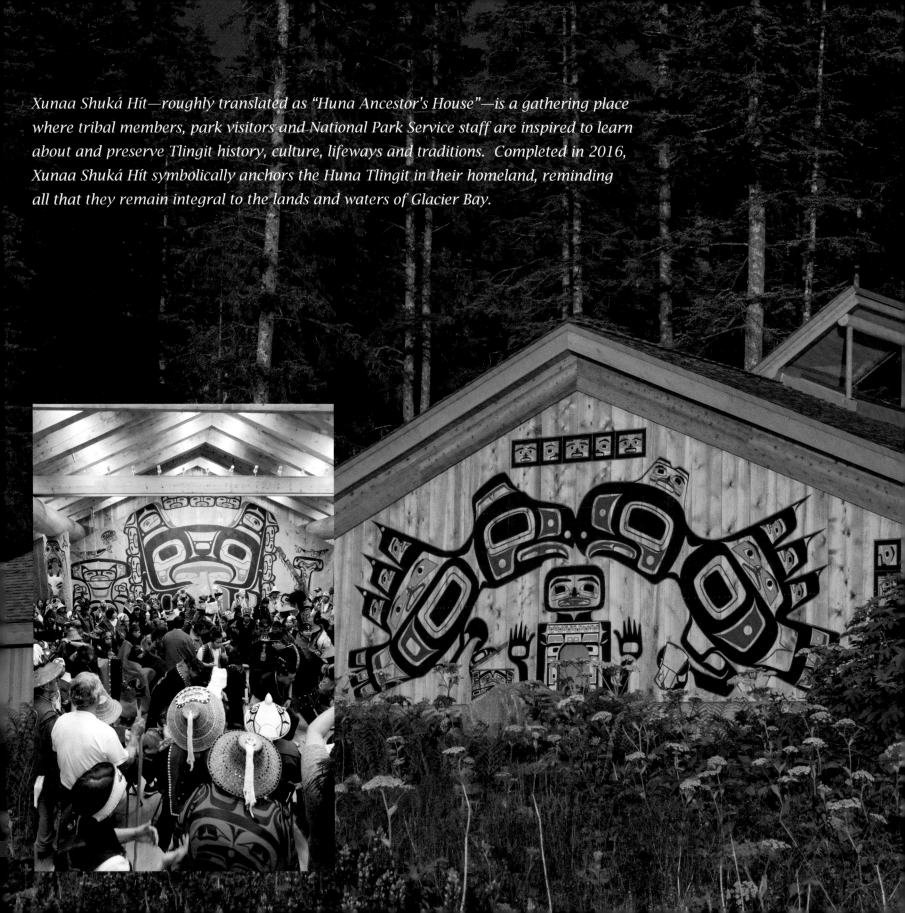

Xunaa Shuká Hít—roughly translated as "Huna Ancestor's House"—is a gathering place where tribal members, park visitors and National Park Service staff are inspired to learn about and preserve Tlingit history, culture, lifeways and traditions. Completed in 2016, Xunaa Shuká Hít symbolically anchors the Huna Tlingit in their homeland, reminding all that they remain integral to the lands and waters of Glacier Bay.

Maintaining Traditions

Over the years in Alaska, more ships came and went: Russian, Spanish, British, American. They increased in frequency and stayed longer, bringing people who were both enamored of the land and sea and the magnificent size of it all, and tempted by the furs, gold, timber and fish. It was a difficult, tumultuous time for the Tlingits, yet they proved resilient. They survived, though at times it was anything but easy.

Missionaries established schools (with help from the federal government) and, for a while, forbade the Tlingits from speaking their own language, the words that held them together and bonded them deeply with the land and sea. Still, they conducted ceremonies, sometimes in hiding, and practiced their arts and crafts, making blankets and baskets and carving totem poles and canoes. They hunted, fished and gathered their ancient foods, and told stories, mother to daughter,

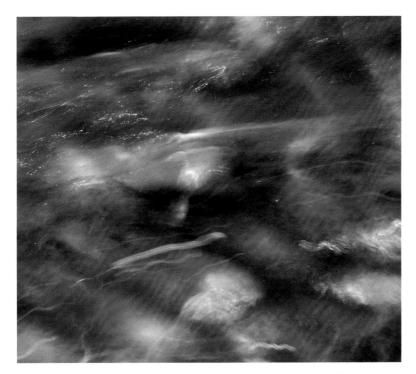

Salmon have returned to the same streams in Glacier Bay for thousands of years, providing a vital food source and spiritual connection for Native people.

uncle to nephew, wise elders to curious children.

Children learned that foods of the land and sea were not taken but received, and that proper thanks were always due. The bones of the first salmon caught each spring were to be returned to the shore so the spirit of the fish could feed them again the following year. The land and sea didn't belong to these people; rather, the people belonged to the land and sea, and they were to leave the world as they found it—bountiful, beautiful, a good place to live. They maintained their ceremonial names, clans and houses, and by doing so, retained their pride and dignity, sometimes by the slimmest of margins.

More than a century before Lapérouse arrived, the Huna Tlingits of Glacier Bay—evicted by the great advancing glacier in the late 1600s—had established a new village, Hoonah, on present-day Chichagof Island, across Icy Strait from the mouth of the bay. But to this day, Glacier Bay remains their ancestral and spiritual homeland, a profoundly important place in their history and sense of being.

As Wayne Howell, former archaeologist and management assistant at Glacier Bay National Park and Preserve, observed, "Some of Glacier Bay's most remarkable riches are its cultures. The Tlingit peoples have lived in this place for sufficient time and in such intimate ways that the forces that have shaped the landscape—earthquakes, giant tsunamis, glaciers—have also shaped the people. The human cultures derived from Glacier Bay's dynamic landscape are every bit as unique to this place as the landscape itself.

"I can stand in a crowd of one thousand Tlingits from throughout Southeast Alaska gathered for Celebration, all dressed in their elaborate regalia, and with little effort, I can spot the people who trace their ancestry to Glacier Bay, to Lituya Bay, to Dry Bay. It is written in the rich art they adorn themselves with, in the songs they sing, in the steps they dance—each nuance in design or movement conveying a story of place."

From Culture to Corporation

The 1959 Alaska Statehood Act specified that a land and resource restitution act be established for the benefit of the Native people. This, together with the 1968 discovery of oil in Prudhoe Bay, motivated the 1971 Alaska Native Claims Settlement Act (ANCSA). A major piece of conservation legislation followed in 1980, when, after considerable debate and compromise between environmentalists, legislators, Native people and business interests, the Alaska National Interest Lands Conservation Act (ANILCA) was passed.

Both ANCSA and ANILCA were unprecedented pieces of lawmaking. The first gave the Native people of Alaska 44 million acres of land (nearly 12 percent of the state) and $1 billion to invest in resource development and other opportunities. It also created 13 Native regional corporations and 203 Native village corporations; each Alaska Native (Inupiat Eskimo, Yupik Eskimo, Athabascan, Aleut, Eyak, Tlingit, Haida and Tsimshian) was an immediate shareholder in his or her village and regional corporation.

Around the world, corporations had become de facto cultures by virtue of their size, influence and durability, but never had aboriginal cultures become instant corporations. ANILCA also made Glacier Bay National Monument into Glacier Bay National Park and Preserve, and enlarged it to 3.3 million acres, an area 50 percent larger than Yellowstone National Park.

Each day, the Huna Tlingits, like all other Alaska Natives, must navigate the difficult waters between their traditional ways; new institutional practices; and the corporate world, with its financial bottom line. Hoonah teenagers play a great game of basketball and spend more time in front of their computers than they do in canoes. Yet, thanks to Celebration and other culturally related activities—including annual visits to Glacier Bay with their parents and elders—the children of Hoonah know who they are. They know where they came from. They know the names of their tribal clans and houses, and their own Tlingit names as well, and the Tlingit names of many places in Glacier Bay. In Hoonah, they sing and dance and drum in the old ways. Some hunt deer and catch salmon, and know what it means to have "a Tlingit sense of being."

They cannot hunt in Glacier Bay as their ancestors did now that it's a national park. But thanks to a 1995 Memorandum of Understanding between the Huna Tlingit and the National Park Service (which was renewed in 2010), studies of wildlife populations may one day determine that the Huna Tlingit can once again harvest some gull eggs, as they did in the distant past. They can then share this food with their elders, who might again taste who they once were, if only for a day, a moment, a memory to last the rest of their lives.

Faces of the Future

The spirits of Glacier Bay live on. Today, Lapérouse would find much of coastal Alaska as wild and breathtaking as it was in 1786. But warmer, and with fewer large tidewater glaciers and more human settlements and roads. Glacier Bay in his day was nearly all glacier and no bay, whereas today, the bay is 70 miles long, and many of the glaciers struggle to hold their ground against a changing world. The Tlingits of his day were far from corporate.

Still, in the way they speak and carry themselves, imbued with the knowledge of where they belong, they are the bright faces of the future. A modern Tlingit is not only a shareholder or a businessman, but also a father, mother, teacher and mentor, a son or a daughter who wants children to know who they are, members of the Tlingit nation—to have that sense of belonging and rootedness that fills them with gratitude and pride. ■

Before the Bay A Grassy Homeland

In the late 1600s before the last advance of the glaciers, Glacier Bay was a grassy valley with salmon-rich streams and home to the Tlingit people. They traveled widely from spring through fall to harvest resources needed to last all winter. Their winter village can be seen in the distance from the fish camp. The advancing ice forced the Tlingit from their homes around 1750, but the Tlingit people are resilient. They returned as the ice retreated and today claim Glacier Bay as their spiritual homeland.

What's in a Name?

The great eighteenth-century Swedish taxonomist Carl Linnaeus, who gave us the system of scientific nomenclature we use to identify and organize all of Earth's species, once said, "If you don't know the names, your knowledge of things perishes."

Then as now, knowledge was power.

Taking Linnaeus's dictum and interweaving it with a Tlingit proverb, Ken Grant, a Glacier Bay park management assistant and Tlingit elder in the T'akteintaan Clan, says, *"Lyee sakoowoo saawx' ch'a tleix ee jeedax goox la hash ee koosteeyi,"* meaning, "If you don't know the names, your [Tlingit] way of life will drift away forever."

Share a name with an elder and he'll likely say with a smile, "Oh, yeah, I remember that one. That's a good one." From the name comes the story, and from the story, history—how a place was used and honored, what kind of foods were found there, and during what time of the year.

"Something that was always there but still delightfully surprised me about many of these names," says Grant, "was the lowercase letter 'i' at the end. It makes the place possessive. Not just for people, but for all things. *Ghaat heeni* isn't just the Sockeye River. The *i* means it's 'the river that belongs to the sockeye salmon.' Without that river, the sockeye wouldn't be there, and without the sockeye, neither would we."

Any one thing depends on everything else. It's a great cycle, a continuum of water, ice, storms and life. The glacier flows from the mountains that rise high into the sky to catch storms fed by moisture lifting off the ocean that ebbs and flows with the tides, and is constantly rejuvenated by the cold waters of the river.

As aboriginal languages disappear around the world, with them go great knowledge and wisdom. The National Park Service in Glacier Bay works closely with the Huna Tlingit to revive every name they can, and to add them to the map of Tlingit place names. Every name evokes memories and storylines that give Glacier Bay even greater significance. As each name is added to the others, a whole new chapter of history is written, reminding us that people have lived here for generations. Fathers and sons stood waist-deep in a cold river and speared salmon, while mothers and daughters dried fish on shore and grandmothers picked berries with their grandchildren—all deeply at home in the only home they'd ever known.

Kugwaas' | Fog

Taan | **Sea lion**

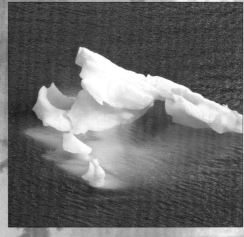

Xaatl | **Iceberg**

Sít tuxóodzi | **Glacier bear**

Dákde at
Offshore wind

Sít'tu Xóodzi
Glacier bear

Dis
Moon

Sit'
Glacier

Haat
Strong incoming
or outgoing tide

T'a
King salmon

Káxwaan
Frost

Taan
Sea lion

Ḵees'
Flooding tide

Te Ḵaas'
Crevasse

Kugwáas'
Fog

Xaatl
Iceberg

L'ook
Silver salmon

Xoots
Brown/grizzly bear

Lein
Tide flats at low tide

Yaay
Whale

S'eek
Black bear

Yánde at
Onshore wind

S'uḵḵasdúk
Very large brown bear

Yeil
Raven

Seew
Rain

Language
of the Land

Place Names

Vivid Lake
Áak'w Kakúxti
Dried Up Little Lake

Icy Strait
S'ix' Tlein
Big Dish (Place of Abundance)

Hugh Miller Inlet
Anáxhkhuyaawal'ix'i Ye
Where Glacier Ice Broke Through

Willoughby Island
Shaltláax̱h Tlein
Big Rock Island Covered with Lichen

South Marble Island
Íxde Neix̱' Xáat'i
South Marble Island

Glacier Bay
Sit' Eeti G̱eiyí
The Bay in Place of the Glacier

Gloomy Knob
Jánwu Aaní
Mountain Goat Land

Grand Pacific Glacier
Sit' Tlein
Grand Glacier

Strawberry Island
Ľeiw x'aat'i
Glacier Sand Island

Geikie Inlet
Wudzidughu Ye
The Area of Many Cottonwood Trees

Muir Inlet
La.áayi Túk̲yee
Area Below the Rising Lake

Beardslee Islands
X'áat'x'i X̱oo
Among the Islands

North Marble Island
Nándei Neix̱' Xáat'i
Going Up Island

Hoonah
Xúniyaa
Lee of the North Wind

Íxde Neix̱' Xáat'i | South Marble Island

Ever since I was a boy, I have heard the names of different points,
bays, islands, mountains, places where [we] get herring, [hunt],
and make camps; that is why I think this country belongs to us.
— Kadashan, Tlingit Leader

Xúniyaa | Hoonah

X'áat'x'i Xoo | Beardslee Islands

S'ix' Tlein | Icy Strait

Heart

Everything is held together by stories.
    —Barry Lopez

After two months with the 1899 Harriman Expedition, geographer Henry Gannett concluded that, yes, Alaska had much to offer in the way of mineral resources—gold, copper and coal—and would no doubt attract prospectors who would create ramshackle waterfront settlements on Alaska's coasts and rivers. And yes, it had much timber, and probably oil. But, remembering Yellowstone and Yosemite national parks, Gannett asserted, "For the one Yosemite of California, Alaska has hundreds." What are we to do with them?

Perhaps hoping that his fellow citizens would restrain themselves, he boldly predicted, "The Alaska coast is to become the showplace of the earth, and pilgrims, not only from the United States, but from far beyond the seas, will throng in endless procession to see it. Its grandeur is more valuable than the gold or the fish or the timber, for it will never be exhausted. This value, measured in direct returns in money received from tourists, will be enormous; measured by health and pleasure, it will be incalculable."

A City Afloat

Gannet was right. Alaska runs neck and neck with the Caribbean as the most popular cruising destination. Today, on any summer day, cruise ships collectively comprise the equivalent of the third largest city in Alaska, measured by the numbers of people they bring and the energy they consume. Wanting to see an America that used to be, visitors flood north, and in Glacier Bay, they find the only coastal national park in Alaska where the park boundary extends into the water rather than ending at the mean high tide line, as it does in Wrangell-St. Elias, Kenai Fjords, Lake Clark and Katmai national parks. Consequently, Glacier Bay National Park and Preserve is the only piece of wild coastal Alaska that limits the

Margerie Glacier's tidewater face is roughly a mile wide and 250 feet high, dwarfing a passenger cruise ship.

numbers of vessels (cruise ships, tour boats and private motorized craft) and manages the ocean environment to give boaters a sense of solitude.

If any place qualifies to become the first designated national marine reserve in Alaska, it's Glacier Bay, given its ecological rebirth and resilience, and the fact that a 2005 U.S. Supreme Court decision recognized the federal government's (not the state of Alaska's) jurisdiction over the waters of the bay.

As far as its value to science, according to ecologist Lewis Sharman, Glacier Bay "is the gift that keeps on giving. Look at the decades of continuous research here, the academic cohorts, [from] graduate students to post-docs to professors who then mentor new generations of curious students. And where do they seem to always return? One guess. Glacier Bay. I know of few places that are as scientifically inspiring, where that inspiration has become manifest in such a powerful legacy of scholarly pursuit."

Wild Music

Sitka-based author and anthropologist Richard Nelson believes Glacier Bay has one of the richest—if not the richest—soundscapes in Alaska. It's a treasure trove of natural sounds, filled with timbre, tone and diversity; a full chorus of bird songs and calls, plus mammals on shore and in the sea; glaciers groaning, crashing and whispering; ice popping and snapping; tides running; rain dripping. So many magnificent and mysterious sounds that carry over the water like wind moving over a wing. "It's a symphony," Nelson says. "Camp one night in Glacier Bay in the peak of summer and it's wild music from dusk to dawn and all day long. It's the Earth singing her song. I've never heard anything more beautiful."

Consider the world of the whale. Whereas people are largely visual animals, whales operate by sound (as do other marine mammals, such as harbor porpoises, harbor seals and, to a lesser degree, Steller sea lions). "In a nutshell," says whale biologist Christine

Pigeon guillemots, diving birds in the Alcid family, are closely related to puffins, auklets, murrelets and murres.

Seeing a humpback whale in Glacier Bay is an experience many visitors never forget. These endangered giants are 40-50 feet (12-16m) long and weigh 40 tons (36,000kg). Humpback whales get their name from their typical diving pattern—arching their back before their final or terminal dive.

Gilman Glacier cascades into Johns Hopkins Inlet as a kayaker maneuvers through the ice. As glacial ice melts it provides a symphony of snaps, crackles and pops.

Gabriele, "the acoustic environment is as important to whales as the trees are to birds. Trees make it possible for birds to do what they do. In the same way, a quiet underwater sound environment makes it possible for whales to do what they do. If you or I were to close our eyes and try to go about our daily activities, it would be really difficult because we rely on our eyesight.

"A whale would have much less of a problem, because they use their hearing for most things where a human would use vision. Although the scientific details of whale hearing are not well understood, we know that they are acoustically adept and rely on sound for basic life functions such as feeding, finding mates, detecting predators and maintaining social bonds."

Aerial view of 15,300-foot Mount Fairweather catching the last light of sunset.

Monitoring the Water World

According to Gabriele, underwater sound monitoring, which has been going on since 2000, "makes it possible to experience the world from the whale's perspective. The National Park Service has a role in protecting the whale's acoustic habitat [underwater sound environment] because it manages the amount of vessel traffic that comes into Glacier Bay.

"When vessel sound takes over the acoustic environment, it's like a fog bank coming in that obscures your ability to see your surroundings. It becomes more difficult to know where you are, find your friends or continue what you were doing. If a male humpback is singing to advertise for a mate but the background noise is so high that other whales can't detect or recognize his song, then he's wasting his time. Whales in today's ocean environments experience this temporary habitat loss many times each day. Marine reserves like Glacier Bay National Park have a special role as natural laboratories that can foster an improved understanding of man-made noise and creative approaches to reducing its effects on marine life."

Keeping an Eye on Climate

Climate change is also an important subject to study in Glacier Bay. The best science available predicts that global climate change will create warmer, wetter conditions in this region of the world, and precipitation will increase in high coastal mountains such as the Fairweather Range.

How will that affect the glaciers? If precipitation that once fell as snow when temperatures were colder now falls as rain, the glaciers will likely thin out and retreat. If the precipitation falls as snow, the glaciers could hold their positions, or even advance. Over tens of thousands of years, glaciers have advanced and retreated again and again in Glacier Bay, at times filling the entire bay and reaching well into Icy Strait, as happened in the early 1700s. At other times, they've retreated to positions similar to those they occupy today.

Heart

In many ways, climate change is a constant. It has transformed landscapes around the world, and in Glacier Bay has sent massive rivers of ice marching forward and falling back. Habitats disappeared. Species shifted. Today, however, the game is different than in the past. Our climate is changing not only as part of a natural oscillation but also as a result of two-and-a-half centuries of humans burning coal and oil that result in greenhouse gases. Levels of atmospheric carbon dioxide (CO_2), measured in ice cores and other corroborating sources, are higher today than they have been any time in the last 650,000 years. Temperatures worldwide are thought to be higher now than they have been since accurate recordkeeping began almost one hundred years ago. The best science out there says the overall warming trend will continue.

"One of the most precious values of the national parks is their ability to teach us about ourselves and how we relate to the natural world," says Jon Jarvis, director of the National Park Service. "This important role may prove invaluable in the near future as we strive to understand and adapt to a changing climate."

Falling in Love with the Land

Scientists and naturalists arrive in Glacier Bay filled with questions, and some never leave. Others fall in love with the area and make their homes here, establishing careers in Glacier Bay, or perhaps in nearby Juneau or elsewhere in Alaska. Tom VandenBerg, who worked as a seasonal ranger-naturalist in Glacier Bay in the early 1990s, jumped at the chance to come back 15 years later to mentor new rangers and live year-round in Gustavus. "Unlike my other moves [to other national park sites], this one was a comfortable homecoming sprinkled with old friends, warm memories and familiar landmarks. The greatest thrill, however, has been raising my two daughters here and watching them grow up amid the meadows, beaches and waters of this remarkable place."

Lewis Sharman concurs. "This place changed my life. Alabama-born and bred, I'd been angling to come to Glacier Bay for years, and when I finally paddled here from Juneau in my crummy little 13-foot whitewater kayak 30 years ago, I did what most folks do. I stood up and stretched and took a good look around. I took a deep breath. I wondered.

"That first summer, I studied black bears, counted harbor seals and described marine intertidal communities. I came to understand and fully appreciate the legacy of scientific work here; the physical and biological diversity; the ever-changing and unending cycle of disturbance and recovery; and the incredible variety of gut-grabbing, interesting questions this place offers to a fledgling scientist. By the end of that summer, I was blindingly fascinated with the theory of plant succession. I spent the next several years teasing apart a few of the stories of how succession occurs in the marine environment following glacial recession.

A natural hole in an iceberg provides a window to the West Arm of Glacier Bay.

"Now I help coordinate the work of other researchers at Glacier Bay, which for me is about the best job in the world. But I still count shoreline-nesting birds, I still keep track of developing plant communities as they age (along with me!), I still monitor oceanographic parameters to better understand the bay's amazingly productive biological cycles. But what I really do is dream about what the heck is going on out there, in the forest, beneath the water. Usually in the context of the change and dynamism that make this place one-of-a-kind.

"I stand up and stretch and take a good look around. I take a deep breath.

"And I wonder. Still."

Cruise ship passengers line the rail to view the face of Margerie Glacier, one of the park's most active tidewater glaciers.

If Glacier Bay were music, it would be an unfinished symphony. If it were a painting, it would be a watercolor. If it were a resolution, it would be a challenge to us all to slow down and sleep on the ground now and then, to take a minute to look, really look, and listen, and to imagine all that's possible when nature isn't a commodity we own, but rather, a community to which we belong.

On any given summer day, lives are changed in Glacier Bay. People find themselves breathless with fascination and gratitude, listening to the land and sea in ways they never have before. It's the same for a hiker on a forest trail in Bartlett Cove, a solo kayaker in the Beardslee Islands or a guest on an expedition tour boat near the seabird colonies of South Marble Island. For a cruise ship passenger witnessing his or her first tidewater glacier or a Tlingit child feeling a bone-deep sense of belonging. For a first-year park ranger knowing that one summer in Glacier Bay has ruined him forever, that other national parks "down south" will never again be as big or wild as they once seemed. The place affects all who encounter it.

The profound beauty, wildness and magnitude of Glacier Bay not only touches people, it transforms them. It provokes and inspires and opens hearts, and gives those who experience it lasting memories and stories. It brings them alive in ways they've never been before, face to face with the ice age and their own distant past, their national park—an American idea, perhaps our best idea, as filmmaker Ken Burns says.

Through deep commitment and steady stewardship, the National Park Service aims to keep the park pristine, to preserve the land and sea uncrowded and undefiled, so future generations will experience the same magic found in Glacier Bay today: the sights, the sounds, the music and majesty of Nature, the purity of it all that enriches anybody who takes a minute to breathe deeply and soak it up. ■

Glacier Glossary

Arete: A high, knife-edged mountain ridge made sharp by glacial erosion on both sides.

Bergy bit: A small iceberg that rises 1 to 4 meters (approximately 3 to 13 feet) out of the water. Bergy bits are dangerous to shipping because they're harder to see than icebergs.

Bergy seltzer: The fizzing "snap, crackle, pop" sound made when air trapped under pressure escapes from bubbles in glacier ice (most often when the ice is floating in water). Also known as ice sizzle.

Crevasse: A crack on the surface of a glacier, created by movement and rapid fracturing of the brittle ice, most often when a glacier makes sharp topographic turns or flows over knobs of resistant bedrock.

Esker: A sinuous, narrow deposit of gravel and smaller sediments made by a meltwater tunnel stream beneath a glacier, visible after the glacier retreats.

Growler: Small chunks of floating ice that rise only about 1 meter (a little more than 3 feet) out of the water.

Iceberg: Pieces of floating ice that rise more than 4 meters (13 feet) out of the water, calved off the face (terminus) of a tidewater glacier.

Icefield: An extensive area of glaciers interconnected at their sources. Southeast Alaska has three icefields: the Stikine, which gives birth to the Le Conte Glacier near Petersburg, the southern-most tidewater glacier in Alaska; the Juneau, due north of Juneau and Lynn Canal; and the Brady, in Glacier Bay National Park, nestled below the Fairweather Range. Reid and Lamplugh Glaciers, in the upper West Arm of the bay, flow from the Brady Icefield.

Moraine: Gravel, boulders and sediments carried on the surface of a glacier, on its flanks (a lateral moraine) or as dark stripes down the middle (a medial moraine); deposited off the end of the glacier at its farthest reach (a terminal moraine) or where the glacier sits for a time as it retreats in stages (a recessional moraine). To the trained eye, moraines reveal a lot about the health and history of a glacier, where it's been, and how long it was there. In Glacier Bay, a terminal moraine (a low, forested ridge) separates Bartlett Cove from Gustavus.

Moulin: A conduit through which meltwater, formed on a glacier's surface, flows down into the interior and/or along the bottom of the glacier.

Serac: A column or tower of glacial ice created by crevasses on all sides.

Tidewater glacier: A glacier that terminates in the ocean, often with a high, vertical face that calves tall towers of ice (seracs) into the sea. Calving is much more frequent in summer than in winter.